OUR · WORLD · MY · ROOTS
JAMAICA

WRITTEN BY ANNA MAKANDA & SHARMANE BARRETT
ILLUSTRATED BY NATÀLIA JUAN ABELLÓ

OUR DEDICATIONS

In Anna's words:

To my parents, for always believing in me and encouraging me to shoot for the moon. To my mum, for teaching me that in order to know who you are, you must know where you come from. To my husband, for being my absolute rock through thick and thin. To my two beautiful children, who inspire me every day. And to my wonderful Jamaican Dad (in law) this one's for you.

In Sharmane's words:

To my parents and my sisters for being my biggest challengers, as well as supporters in life. To my nine amazing nieces and nephews, for being my constant reminder that I need to be a better me for all of the little eyes that are watching. And in honour of my late Jamaican grandparents who experienced significant hardship to pursue a better life for us; those sacrifices were not made in vain.

To all the little explorers,
may you always remember to:

BE CURIOUS

BE CONFIDENT

BE KIND

BE YOU

CONTENTS

FACTFILE — 01

MAP OF JAMAICA — 03

INTRO — 05

HELLO — 07

WELCOME — 09

MEET MY FAMILY — 11

WHERE WE LIVE — 13

LET'S EXPLORE — 15

LET'S GO TO SCHOOL — 27

LET'S PLAY	31
LET'S SAY	33
LET'S EAT	35
LET'S CELEBRATE	37
LET'S TELL A STORY	43
LET'S GET LUCKY	45
LET'S DREAM	47
GOODBYE	51
FLAG	53
HISTORY	54

ASIA

NORTH AMERICA

JAMA

OCEANIA

SOUTH AMERICA

ANTARCTICA

LOCATION
Jamaica is an island country in the Caribbean Sea. The closest island to the north is Cuba, and the closest island to the east is Hispaniola (Haiti and the Dominican Republic).
Size: 10,991 km². It is the third-largest island in the Caribbean (after Cuba and Hispaniola).
Capital: Kingston 🔍
Currency: Jamaican Dollar (JMD)
Population: 2.7 million (2020)
Originally the country was inhabited by the native Arawak and Taino people, but following the arrival of the explorer, Christopher Columbus, this changed. It is now 90% black or black mixed (traced back to West Africa), with white, Indian, and Chinese Jamaicans. Our motto is: 'Out of many, one people'.
Major Cities: Spanish Town, Portmore, Montego Bay 🔍
Parishes: There are 14 parishes in Jamaica: Clarendon, Hanover, Kingston, Manchester, Portland, Saint Andrew, Saint Ann, Saint Catherine, Saint Elizabeth, Saint James, Saint Mary, Saint Thomas, Trelawny, Westmoreland
Highest Point: Blue Mountain Peak at 2,256 m

WEATHER
Jamaica has a hot and humid tropical climate where the temperature ranges between 21 and 33°C. There are four seasons:
Wet season 1: May-June
Hot season: July-August
Wet season 2: September-November
Cooler season: December-April
The island lies in the 'hurricane belt' of the Atlantic Ocean, so it frequently suffers significant storm damage.

LANGUAGES
English is the official language. Informally, people speak Jamaican patois or Patwa, which is a colourful mix of several languages passed down from ancestors.

RELIGION
69% of the population in Jamaica is Christian (of varying denominations). The remainder is a mix of Muslim, Hindu, Buddhist, Jewish, or Rastafarian, and some who consider themselves to have no religious beliefs.

DOLPHIN COVE

DUNN'S RIVER FALLS

JUAN DE BOLAS MOUNTAINS

KINGSTON

BLUE MOUNTAINS

JOHN CROW MOUNTAINS

SPANISH TOWN

PORTMORE

PORT ROYAL

REGGAE FALLS

KEEP AN EYE OUT FOR

- Capital: Kingston
- Major Cities: Spanish Town, Portmore, Montego Bay
- Mountains: Blue, John Crow, Juan de Volas, Mocho
- Rivers: Black, Rio Minho, Martha Brae
- Waterfalls: Dunn's River, YS Falls
- Limestone Hills
- Dolphin Cove
- Blue Lagoon
- Port Royal

ARE YOU EXCITED ABOUT GOING ON AN ADVENTURE?

Join us on a journey across land and sea, taking you to Jamaica, the land of wood and water, once known to its natives as 'Xaymeca'. It is a Caribbean island rich with fruits and spices, with a landscape that ranges from soaring mountains and tropical rainforests to sprawling meadowlands and dramatic coastlines. This book will guide you through the country's geography, people, culture, and beyond.

But there's more there than meets the eye: Jamaica has a diversity of communities and traditions. The people of Jamaica are known for having a carefree warmth. They pride themselves on being very entertaining – the life of the party.

You may be surprised to find that even though Jamaica is filled with lots of things that are different to where you live, there are many similarities too.

Jamaica is about 22 times smaller than England and home to over 2.5 million people who have different ethnicities, languages, and religions.

Perhaps you have Jamaican heritage and you want to learn more about your roots, or simply want to learn more about this amazing country. You will find some of the many special things about Jamaica in this book, but there is so much more to discover. We hope that you will be able to travel all the way to Jamaica and beyond someday.

THE OFFICIAL LANGUAGE OF JAMAICA IS ENGLISH.

Informally, most Jamaican's speak Patwa.

HELLO

HOWDY
(PATWA)

WAGWAN
(PATWA)

ELLO
(PATWA)

GREETINGS
(PATWA)

HAIL UP
(PATWA)

WADADA
(PATWA)

OYEE
(PATWA)

MEET MY FAMILY

I live with my mum and dad, three brothers and two sisters. We speak Patwa and English. I have many aunts, uncles, and cousins too, as my mum has nine brothers and sisters, and my dad has seven.

Dad
Fahda

Mum
Madda

Grandma
Granny
(Grandmadda)

Grandad
Pupa
(Grandfahda)

Brother
Bredda

Sister
Sistah

ZIGGY LIVES WITH HIS FAMILY IN THE NEIGHBOURHOOD.

They also speak Patwa and English.

We call Ziggy's mum and dad (and any adults older than my parents) 'Mr and Miss'. My dad says that this is the way we show our respect to those who are older than us.

DID YOU KNOW?

Jamaicans often give a child a name based on the day or occasion they were born. Another trend is to give a name that represents a good quality. Many of these names are rooted in religion. This is what our names represent:

Tashelle – Born on Christmas Day
Shenice – God is gracious and merciful
Ziggy – Victory, protection

Nicknames (pet names) are used a lot – nearly everyone has one.

WHERE WE LIVE

Ziggy and I both live in a bungalow in the parish of Clarendon. We can see magnificent sunset views at Portland Ridge which is very close to our home.

My cousins, Kalisa and Omari, live in a gated apartment complex in Kingston.

Kalisa & Omari's home

Granny and Pupa live in a small bungalow in the parish of St Elizabeth, where there is a lot of luscious greenery.

Granny & Pupa's bungalow

LET'S EXPLORE

LANDSCAPES

Shen and I love visiting different parts of Jamaica. Every now and then, Fahda will take the family on a drive for the day and it is always an adventure. We can see some amazing views. There are over 50 beaches in Jamaica and so sometimes we stop to cool off in the sea. Here are some of the things we have seen along the way:

MOUNTAINS

There are 15 mountains in Jamaica and many hills. The Blue Mountains make up the longest mountain range in Jamaica and they include the island's highest point, Blue Mountain Peak.

DID YOU KNOW?

The Blue Mountains are named after the mist that covers this mountain range. From a distance, this gentle mist actually appears to be blue.

OTHER WELL-KNOWN MOUNTAINS ARE...

John Crow Mountains   Juan de Volas Mountains   Mocho Mountains

FORESTS

Jamaica was originally deeply forested, but in parts of the island the forests have now been removed. The forests that are left are full of ferns as well as bamboo, ebony, and mahogany trees. There are also many tropical dry forests in the limestone hills in the south of Jamaica.

RIVERS

There are over 120 rivers in Jamaica, many unexplored and unreachable. The two main ones are the Black River and the Rio Minho. There are also rivers, like the Martha Brae, that are popular for rafting.

The Black River is the widest river in Jamaica. The river ends in the Caribbean Sea at Black River Town.
Q: How many Hammerhead sharks long is the Black River?
A: 8,900 Hammerhead shark's long – 53.4 km long

The Rio Minho is not as wide as the Black River, but it is the longest river in Jamaica. It starts in the mountains near Spaldings, flows through the southwest of the country, and reaches the Caribbean Sea at Carlisle Bay.
Q: How many Hammerhead sharks long is the Rio Minho?
A: 15,467 Hammerhead shark's long – 92.8 km long

WATERFALLS

Jamaica has many waterfalls which are popular amongst tourists. These include Dunn's River Falls, Reggae Falls, Reach Falls, and Cane River Falls. Many have a jungle trek to get to the top before you can see the beautiful views. If you are lucky, you can spend the day swimming in the cold pools at the bottom. The largest and most famous waterfall is Dunn's River Falls.

WETLANDS

There are many areas of wetland in the south of Jamaica where plants and animals have adapted to permanent flooding.

It is possible to tour the wetlands on a swamp safari, where you will see animals such as crocodiles, snakes, and iguanas, as well as over 100 species of birds.

PLANTS AND TREES

There are thousands of different types of plants and trees in Jamaica. Shen loves the bull hoof, the cannon ball, and the golden shower trees because she thinks their names are cool. My favourite is the avocado pear tree because I LOVE avocados – especially when I eat them with bulla and cheese.

MANGROVE TREE

A mangrove is a shrub or small tree that grows in coastal salt water. Mangroves split their lives between land and sea, protecting the shoreline. There are four types of mangroves: red, black, white, and button. Mangroves provide shelter for hundreds of endangered species including sea horses, sea turtles, stingrays, pelicans, groupers, and mutton snappers.

They play a key role in acting as a barrier to protect Jamaica against floods, strong waves, and high winds during storms. They are threatened by hurricanes and invasive species e.g. rats and humans. People are now trying really hard to protect them.

Jamaica is home to about 3,000 species of native flowering plants, thousands of species of non-flowering plants, and twenty botanical gardens.

THE LIGNUM VITAE

This is the national flower of Jamaica, which is native to the island. The name means 'tree of life' or 'wood of life' because this flowering evergreen tree has many medicinal uses. Granny drinks the tea for her sore knees.

DID YOU KNOW?

The *lignum vitae* tree is one of the most useful trees in the world because each part of the tree has a use. The wood has been used for ship propellers, the gum and bark to cure diseases, and the leaves used to clean floors and clothes.

ANIMALS

When Dajuan, Damian, and Deshane (our cousins from England) came to stay, we went on a trip to Dolphin Cove. We explored the jungle trail where there are many wild animals, plants, and trees. We were also able to swim with dolphins in their natural habitat. Dolphins are very intelligent and they sometimes help injured people and other sea life. They have their own whistle to recognise each other. 🔍

DID YOU KNOW?

Dolphins sleep by resting one side of their brains at a time, which allows them to continue rising to the surface for air and to keep an eye open to watch out for predators.

DID YOU KNOW?

Jamaica's national bird is the red-billed streamertail hummingbird.

Jamaica has four species of hummingbird, three of which are not found anywhere else in the world. It's one of the only places where you can feed hummingbirds with sugar and water in a little bottle.

HERE ARE SOME OF THE MANY OTHER ANIMALS AND INSECTS YOU MAY FIND IN JAMAICA – SEE IF YOU CAN SPOT THEM:

Bat, wild boar, small Asian Mongoose, lizard, snake, black-billed parrot, Jamaican blackbird, Jamaican owl, hummingbird, firefly, treefrog, iguana, manatee, flamingo, giant swallowtail butterfly, freshwater turtle, reef fish, nurse shark, eel, hammerhead shark, tiger shark, bull shark.

DUNN'S RIVER FALLS 🔍

Last summer, I visited Dunn's River Falls with Ziggy and his family. It is one of the most famous attractions in Jamaica because it is made up of a series of limestone slopes that are not too steep and act like giant natural stairs. The waterfall is nearly 60 m tall, spans over 182 m and takes over an hour to climb.

DID YOU KNOW?

Dunn's River Falls is one of the few waterfalls in the world to actually flow directly into the sea.

YS FALLS 🔍

The YS Falls is another popular attraction and it has seven tiers. Unlike Dunn's River, you can't climb it, but there are natural pools and several rope swings. When we are big enough, Ziggy and I want to zipline over the Falls.

BLUE LAGOON 🔍

Ziggy and I also went on a school trip here. It is Jamaica's largest underground spring-fed lagoon, which has a mix of hot and cold fresh water and salt water. It made our skin feel tingly. Some people say that the Blue Lagoon is bottomless, but in reality, it is almost 60 m deep and fed by fresh, glistening, turquoise-blue mineral water and surrounded by lush green vegetation.

PORT ROYAL 🔍

Port Royal was the original centre of shipping and commerce in the Caribbean in the late 17th century. It was destroyed by several severe earthquakes and continues to be damaged by hurricanes. Granny loves to tell us the stories she was told by her mother, of the pirates who came from Africa and spent their gold and treasures in the town.

DID YOU KNOW?

Port Royal was once called *'the richest and wickedest city in the world'*. The notorious pirate, Captain Morgan, lived there and made lots of raids on land and sea. Rumour has it that some of Captain Morgan's treasures are still hidden in the caves nearby.

LET'S GO TO SCHOOL

Ziggy, Shen, and I go to the same primary school in Clarendon. We are in third grade.

Our school is big with many classrooms. There are lots of fields where we run around and play sports. Each day we catch the school bus to and from school.

Our cousin, Iriye, lives in the rural area of Portland. Her school is quite different to ours as it is much smaller with only three classrooms – one for each grade. She tells us it can get very full as everyone tries to squeeze in. She walks a long way to and from school.

This year, I made it onto the school quiz team and I am hoping to win 'quiz champ' in the televised quiz competition. We always have a lot of homework to do – it takes us about two hours every day and sometimes a lot longer at weekends. We also have to learn the National Anthem and the National School Song by heart, as well as our times tables and The Lord's Prayer.

WE HAVE THE MOST FUN IN OUR...

MUSIC LESSONS

We play these instruments:

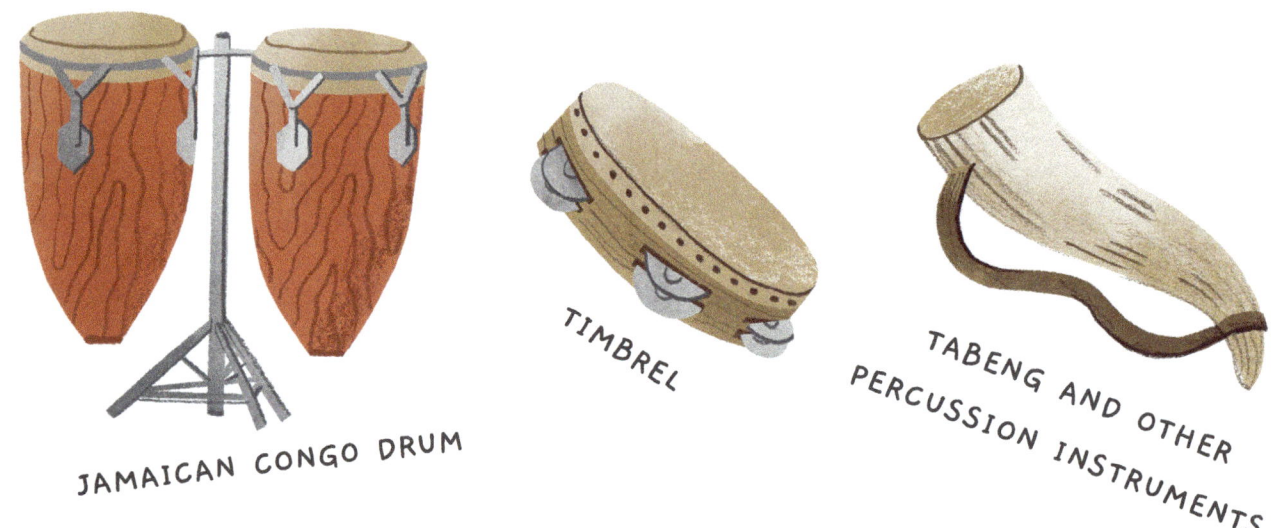

JAMAICAN CONGO DRUM

TIMBREL

TABENG AND OTHER PERCUSSION INSTRUMENTS

Shen loves to sing and she has a really lovely voice. I wish I could sing too, but I have been learning to play the harp for two years. Ziggy loves to try different instruments and he is very good at playing the guitar.

PE LESSONS

At school, we play lots of different sports, but soccer, cricket, and track and field are the most popular. All of the boys want to be like Usain Bolt, and the girls want to be like Shelly-Ann Fraser-Pryce.

We all love it when the Olympics is on because we go with our families to our favourite bar in the town centre to watch the track and field. Everyone is very animated supporting Jamaica and the crowd goes wild when we win. Shen and I make up a victory dance.

DID YOU KNOW?

Jamaica was the first tropical country to send a bobsledding team to the Winter Olympics in 1988. A popular film was made about this: *Cool Runnings*.

Also, Jamaica is home to the fastest person on the planet – Usain Bolt.

LET'S PLAY

In the playground at school, one of my favourite games to play is 'Stucky Freezy'. My cousins Dajuan, Damian, and Deshane say that this game is called 'Simon Says' in the UK. Granny also taught us to play...

WHAT CAN YOU DO, PUNCIENELLA LIKKLE FELLA?

Players: 3+

One player is chosen to be 'Puncienella'. Everyone else claps their hands in a ring around them and sings 'What can you do, Puncienella likkle fella?' Puncienella then stops and performs an action. The other players copy the action while singing, 'We can do it too, Puncienella likkle fella'. Whomever Puncienella stops in front of becomes the next Puncienella.

LET'S SAY

Here are some of our everyday words and phrases in Jamaican Patwa. Why not try and say them?

MI NAME
MY NAME IS

GUD MAWNIN
GOOD MORNING

GUD NITE
GOOD NIGHT

GUD AFTANOON
GOOD AFTERNOON

MI LUV YUH
I LOVE YOU

MI BEG YUH
PLEASE

TANK YUH
THANK YOU

WEH YUH AH SEH?
WHAT ARE YOU SAYING?

MI DEH YAH, YUH KNOW
EVERYTHING IS OK

BIG UP
WELL DONE

MI SOON COME
I'LL BE RIGHT THERE

LET'S EAT

FOOD & DRINK

We are always really hungry when we wake up, Madda makes us cornmeal porridge most mornings. Every Friday, we get a special breakfast of ackee and saltfish, with bammy and steamed cabbage.

At dinner-time Fahda cooks curry chicken with rice and peas. We often have it with sweet potatoes, yams, breadfruit, and green bananas instead of rice. He also makes my favourite – chicken-foot soup. Yum!

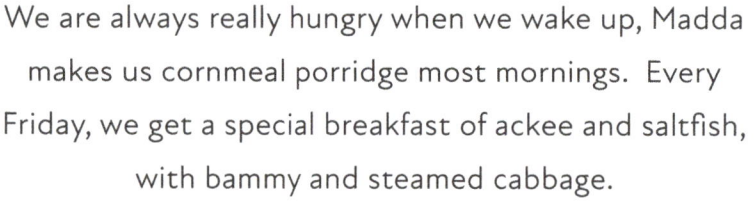

We snack on lots of sugarcane. Ziggy has mango and jackfruit trees in his garden so his Madda, Miss Olive, brings us lots of fruit. Shen loves jelly coconuts, especially when Pupa climbs the coconut tree to pick them for her. She always giggles when she tells the story of the time when she was playing with our other brothers and sisters, and one fell out of the tree and hit her on the head. She was okay, but it can be dangerous.

Sometimes Madda lets us have a sweet treat. Our favourite is coconut drops. Granny will bake us grater cake for a special treat, which is actually not a cake, but grated coconut mixed with sugar and water. Usually the top is coloured pink. It's delicious!

We drink sinkle bible tea every morning which is a tea made with aloe vera. We don't like it, but Pupa says we must drink it because it is good for us. We could drink box juice all day though. We aren't allowed to drink carrot or Guinness punch because Madda says that we are too young.

NATIONAL HOLIDAYS

We celebrate special national holidays in Jamaica. Pupa says that we have these days to honour important events and people in history. We have:

6th February – Bob Marley Day – a day to celebrate the birthday of Bob Marley. Typically, four days of music festivals are held in St Anne, Bob Marley's birth-place, to celebrate the reggae icon.

23rd May – Labour Day – a day to celebrate the achievement of workers.

6th August – Independence Day – a day to celebrate Jamaica gaining independence from British rule in 1962 after 300 years.

Every third Monday in October – a day to remember seven national heroes whose heroic deeds led to greater freedom and social betterment for Jamaica.

LET'S CELEBRATE

We LOVE to celebrate. We get together with family and friends. Ziggy and I get dressed up, eat tasty food, listen to music, and dance all day long.

ANNUAL CELEBRATIONS

Easter Sunday Carnival – people travel from all over the world to celebrate the people of Jamaica, their local customs, and heritage. There are many street parades with masquerade bands and steel bands, live music events, dancing, and competitions. This is a week-long celebration.

22/23rd September – Harvest Festival – an autumn tradition to give thanks for a plentiful crop, the day is filled with fun events for all the family.

26th December and 1st Jan – Junkanoo – a street parade with music, dance, and costumes of mixed African origin, every Boxing Day and New Year's Day.

We also celebrate birthdays and Easter.

CHRISTMAS

Every year, Fahda gets us a Christmas tree and we decorate the house. On Christmas Eve, we are all so excited about the Grand Market. Everyone does their last-minute shopping and we can find unique things that aren't available for the rest of the year.

Most people come out in the evening and it's like a big street party as there is a sound system on every corner, the sound of laughter, the smoke of jerk chicken being grilled, and people rushing to buy gifts. We never get home before midnight and when we do get home, Shen and I find it difficult to sleep because we are so excited.

We always wake up really early on Christmas morning so we can open our presents. We have calypso carols playing in the background and sometimes Fahda will take us to the beach for a few hours to get us out of the house. We enjoy the decorations and the presents, but the best part is the food.

Early in the year, Pupa chooses one of his goats to be fattened up ready to eat on Christmas Day. Granny makes us a huge pot of curried goat as well as mannish water soup.

Fahda gets up early to put a huge leg of ham in the oven to roast and Madda cooks up a real storm. We eat everything with rice and gungo peas (which come into season around Christmas time) and we wash it all down with a big glass of sorrel. Granny also makes a big fruit cake which she soaks in rum for days and she offers it to all of our guests throughout the day. All of the family celebrate together… We love Christmas.

GIVING GIFTS

Madda often gifts ackee to the neighbours because we have some ackee trees in our back yard. Some of our neighbours have pear trees, coconut trees, and banana trees and so in season, they bring them around to share. Madda always says, *'You cyan dead fi hungry,'* because at times there is too much food. Even when there is too much, we must always be thankful.

DRESSING UP

Most of the time we wear the same kind of clothes that Dajuan, Damian, and Deshane wear in the UK. On special occasions, some of our family get dressed up in traditional dress – especially on holidays like Independence Day. It's so much fun to wear long flowing skirts with matching headwraps.

EATING

We often eat curried goat with rice and peas on special occasions. The bigger the occasion, the bigger the dinner that is served, like on Christmas Day.

PLAYING MUSIC

Music plays a really big part in our lives and you can hear it everywhere – on celebration days, street corners, and in everybody's kitchens. Even at home, when Madda is cooking breakfast before we get ready to go out, she dances around the kitchen to music and sings along – it gets us in the party mood. Our favourite types of music are reggae, ska, and rocksteady, as well as gospel. They all have a distinctive island beat.

DANCE

At parties, there is usually reggae or dancehall music playing, and everyone will be dancing. Granny is the best dancer; she dances for hours and will be the last one dancing. She said that sometimes she and her friends have even danced for days on end. There are some dances like the bruckins and jonkonnu which are performed on special days.

LET'S TELL A STORY

We Jamaicans love our traditions and a big part of our culture is storytelling. The stories originated from our African ancestors, passed down from generations. At the weekends, we often stay with Granny and Pupa. We love staying with them because Granny and Pupa take it in turns to tell us a story before bedtime as we sit on the veranda.

Shen's favourite story is about the River Mumma – a water spirit who guards Jamaica's rivers whilst sitting on the riverbanks combing her long hair.

Ziggy told me that he loves the Rolling Calf – a story about a menacing bull haunting the countryside at night.

My favourite is about Anansi the spider – an eight-legged creature, whose mischievous antics get him in and out of trouble. These stories often teach a life lesson such as honesty being the best policy or greed bringing bad luck.

LET'S GET LUCKY

What do you do when your tooth falls out? What are the things that bring good luck? Here are some of ours…

TOOTH

When you lose a tooth, throw it on the rooftop and say, 'Eat rat, take me old teeth and gimme a new one!'

SNEEZING

If someone sneezes, you say, 'bless you', which is a way of asking good spirits to come to them.

GOOD LUCK

If your right palm is itchy, it is a sign that you will receive money, and therefore good luck.
We say, 'mi hand middle a scratch me'.

If your right eye twitches, or is jumping, you are going to laugh.
We say, 'mi right eye a jump'.

If you are lucky enough for a bird to poop on you, then a windfall is imminent.

BAD LUCK

If you walk over spilt salt, bad luck will follow you.

If your left eye twitches, you will hear bad news, or something will make you cry.

If your left palm is itchy, it is a sign that money will leave you, and therefore bad luck.

LET'S DREAM

Sometimes we close our eyes and dream about what we would like to be when we grow up.

Do you know what you would like to be?

I WANT TO BE THE FASTEST WOMAN IN THE WORLD AT SPRINTING. MY FAVOURITE ATHLETES ARE:

SHELLY-ANN FRASER-PRYCE

Shelly-Ann is one of the greatest female sprinters of all time. She is a two-time Olympic gold medallist and a four-time world champion. These are just some of her many achievements. She is nicknamed the 'Pocket Rocket' because she is small and explosive in her start. She has won many awards for her athletic talent. She is also known for having fun and colourful hair.

USAIN BOLT

Bolt was named the 'fastest man alive' after winning three gold medals at the 2008 Olympic games and after becoming the first man in Olympic history to win both the 100- and 200-metre races in record times. He also made history by being the first person to win three gold medals at three Olympic games in a row.

Shen enjoys speaking in public and our parents say that she would make a great politician, like...

PORTIA SIMPSON-MILLER

Portia was Jamaica's first female prime minister. Portia has done a lot for equality and has helped women be recognised for their capabilities and achievements, both in Jamaica and internationally. She is a champion for equality in Jamaica.

Ziggy really enjoys science and says that his dream is to be an inventor, like...

JOEL SADLER

Joel is known for co-inventing the Jaipur Knee: a budget-friendly prosthetic knee joint that has benefited amputees in low-income communities worldwide. Joel also founded a creative computing start-up company with the vision to 'spark every child's inner inventor'. It enables children to build their own computers through a game-based learning platform.

Ziggy also loves playing football with his friends and he dreams of being a footballer, like...

RAHEEM STERLING

Raheem was born in Jamaica but moved to London at the age of 5. He was scouted at the age of 10, and he started playing professional football when he was 17. He currently plays for Manchester City, and he is also part of the England national team.

Raheem has also set up The Raheem Sterling Foundation to educate, empower and inspire young people in Jamaica, the UK and beyond.

WE HOPE THAT YOU HAD FUN EXPLORING JAMAICA WITH US — ZIGGY, SHEN, AND I REALLY ENJOYED SHOWING YOU AROUND. WE HOPE TO SEE YOU BACK SOON.

GOODBYE

MI
GAAN
(PATWA)

INNA DI
MORROWS
(PATWA)

LICKLE
MORE
(PATWA)

National anthem
'Jamaica, Land We Love.'

MEANING OF THE FLAG

The Jamaican flag was unveiled for the first time in 1962 when Jamaica became independent after 300 years of British rule. Here's what the colours represent:

Black	The strength and creativity of the people
Green	The hope and the land itself
Gold	The natural wealth and beauty of sunlight

DID YOU KNOW?

Jamaica is actually one of only two countries in the world that doesn't have red, white, or blue in its flag.

HISTORY

Pre-1494	Jamaica was inhabited by the Arawak tribes
1494	Portuguese explorer, Christopher Columbus arrived
1509-1655	The Spanish enslaved the Arawak and their tribes became extinct by 1600 due to diseases brought to Jamaica by the Spanish
1513-1655	Hundreds of slaves were transported from West Africa
1655	England invaded Jamaica and defeated the Spanish colony
1670	Port Royal became a commercial hub and a home for Captain Henry Morgan
1692	Sugar cane began to replace piracy as Jamaica's main source of income and hundreds of thousands of West African slaves were brought to work on the plantations
1800	The slave population increased to over 300,000
1831	The Baptist War
1834	Slavery was abolished
1865	The Morant Bay Rebellion
1872	Kingston became the capital city of Jamaica
1927-1935	The era of Marcus Garvey, 'the activist'
1930s	The Rastafari Movement
1962	Independence from the UK; Bustamante was appointed Prime Minister
1968	First reggae records released
1988	Hurricane Gilbert hit Jamaica
2005	Jamaica began to dominate 100-m sprint record
2008	Usain Bolt broke three Olympic records, and there was a Jamaican sweep of all medals in the women's 100-m sprint

THE AUTHORS

ANNA MAKANDA

Anna was born in Gweru, Zimbabwe, and raised in London, along with her older sister. Her father is Zimbabwean and her mother, Scottish. Growing up, Anna always dreamed of owning her own business. She started her career as an accountant but soon realised it was time to pursue her dreams. That was when she set up her own fitness brand.
In her spare time, you will find her spending time with family and friends, chasing after her two very energetic children, or writing a book or two!

SHARMANE BARRETT

Sharmane was born and raised in London, along with her five sisters. Her father is Jamaican and her mother, Trinidadian-English. Growing up, Sharmane was encouraged to pursue a career as a lawyer but after completing her legal studies, she soon realised that law was not for her. She began working in legal recruitment, which gave her an opportunity to live in Singapore for almost four years. Sharmane's passions are travelling and boxing – although these days there is a lot less travelling to exotic destinations, and a lot more time in the gym.

THE ILLUSTRATOR

NATÀLIA JUAN ABELLÓ

Natàlia was born in Barcelona, where she grew up with her older brother, father, and mother. She has loved drawing since she was little and was often found creating and daydreaming as a young girl. Pursuing her dream of working in a creative job, she studied to become a fashion designer but very quickly realised her real passion was to illustrate, especially children's books. Natàlia moved to the UK many years ago and now lives in a small countryside village. She loves nature, and she's happiest when taking long hikes with her partner and little doggy.

OUR GRATITUDE

We would like to say thank you and extend our gratitude to:

Everyone who helped us with the research; Anna's cousin Erica and Dad (in law), Sharmane's friend, Trudy for your advice, opinions, and most importantly, time. Thank you.

Our editor, Amber, who helped us make our facts engaging to our young readers; our copywriter Lisa; our proof-reader, Josie; and Martyn, our wonderful designer, who not only made our books look as beautiful as they do but also helped us articulate our vision so perfectly. To our incredibly talented illustrator, Natàlia, for bringing Tashie, Shen, and Ziggy to life, and for showcasing the magic of Jamaica.

And not forgetting all our little people for helping us pick the designs and road-testing the content.

Each other. This is a passion project for us both and to be able to share this journey with a best friend is the dream.

Anna and Sharmane

OUR MISSION

Our mission is to help ignite a child's interest in their roots and empower them to become culturally confident. We aim to do this by providing parents and caregivers factual yet engaging resources to help them teach their children about their culture and heritage.

OUR SOCIAL IMPACT

Children everywhere should have access to education. This is why for every book sold we will be donating a percentage of the proceeds to the OWMR fund which aims to support charities that do exactly that.

COPYRIGHT

First published 2021
Text Copyright ©: Anna Makanda and Sharmane Barrett
Illustration Copyright ©: Natàlia Juan Abelló

Printed in the UK
ISBN: 978-1-7399365-1-8
www.ourworldmyroots.com

All rights reserved. No part of this book may be reproduced in any form by an electronic or mechanical means, including information storage and retrieval systems, without permission in writing from the publisher, except by a reviewer who may quote brief passages in a review.

This is a work of creative nonfiction. Some parts have been fictionalised in varying degrees, for various purposes.

The publishers will be pleased to make good any omissions or rectify any mistakes brought to their attention at the earliest opportunity.

A SPECIAL THANKS TO EESA DENNIS, AGED 9, FOR DRAWING THIS JAMAICAN-INSPIRED PATTERN.

www.ingramcontent.com/pod-product-compliance
Ingram Content Group UK Ltd.
Pitfield, Milton Keynes, MK11 3LW, UK
UKHW050023051225
465748UK00001B/1